HURON COUNTY LIBRARY

S0-CFT-650

DISCARD

HURON COUNTY LIBRARY

Date Due

BPU Oc9 JUL 28 '98		

8441

971	Laforet, Andrea Lynne, 1948-
.1	The book of the Grand Hall / Andrea Laforet. --
004	Hull, Quebec : Canadian Museum of Civilization,
97	c1992.
Laf	79 p. : ill. (some col.)

Includes bibliographical references (p. 79)
0689495X   ISBN:0660140012 (pbk.)

1. Canadian Museum of Civilization - Exhibitions. 2.
Indians of North America - Pacific Coast (B.C.) -
Exhibitions. I. Canadian Museum of Civilization. II. Title

1221   93JUN26   06/he   1-01013576

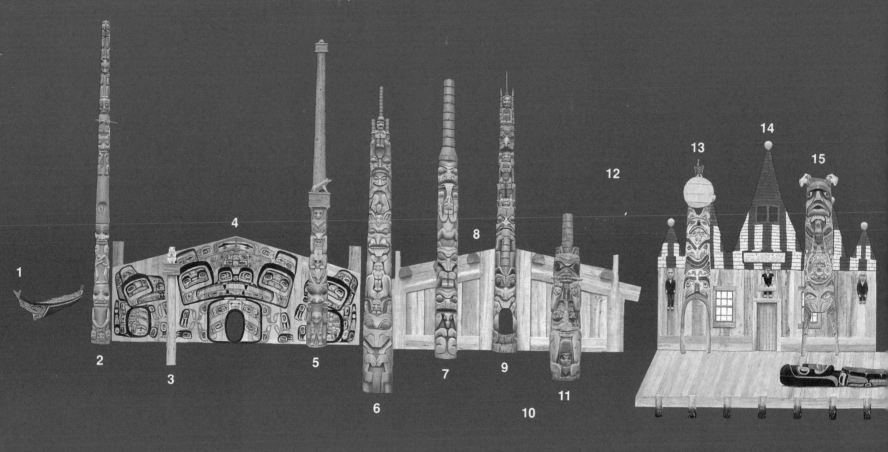

The Grand Hall, 1989 (Drawing: G. Webber)

1. Haida Canoe
2. Bear's Den Pole
3. White Squirrel
4. Tsimshian House
5. Kwahsuh Pole
6. Fox Warren Pole
7. Kayang Pole
8. Haida House
9. House Waiting for Property Pole
10. Estuary Environment
11. Chief Wiah's House Post
12. Forest Environment

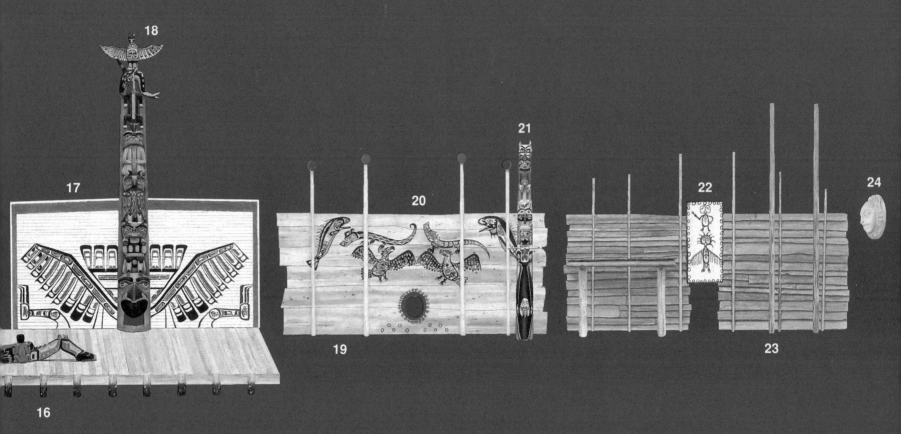

13. Tallio Pole

14. Nuxalk House

15. Chief Qomoqua's Pole

16. Tsonoqua Feast Dish

17. Central Coast House

18. Wakas Pole

19. Summer Shore

20. Nuu-Chah-Nulth House

21. Nuu-Chah-Nulth Pole

22. Coast Salish House

23. Tidal Pool

24. *Raven Bringing Light to the World*

THE BOOK OF THE GRAND HALL

ANDREA LAFORET

CANADIAN MUSEUM
OF CIVILIZATION

JUL 1 5 1993

8441

© 1992 Canadian Museum of Civilization

Canadian Cataloguing in Publication Data

The Book of the Grand Hall

Includes bibliographical references.
ISBN 0-660-14001-2

1. Indians of North America — Pacific Coast (B.C.) —
Exhibitions. 2. Canadian Museum of Civilization —
Exhibitions. I. Laforet, Andrea Lynne, 1948-   .
II. Title.

E78.B9C32 1992   971.1'00497   C92-099556-X

DSS cat. no. NM98-3/75-1992E

Printed and bound in Canada

Published by the
Canadian Museum of Civilization
100 Laurier Street
P.O. Box 3100, Station B
Hull, Quebec
J8X 4H2

Issued also in French under the title:

Le livre de la Grande Galerie
ISBN 0-660-90554-X
DSS cat. no. NM98-3/75-1992F
Publié par le Musée canadien des civilisations

Credits

Managing Editor/Text Editor: Julie Swettenham
Designer: Miriam Bloom, Expression Communications
Production Officer: Deborah Brownrigg

Cover photograph: Harry Foster, Canadian Museum of Civilization, with
  special effects by BGM Photo Centre, Ottawa

Photograph on page 3: The Nahwitti house-entrance figure (Hans Blohm,
  Canadian Museum of Civilization)

Canada

Printed on recycled paper

Contents

Introduction

THE DEVELOPMENT of the Grand Hall exhibit began in 1984 and is still continuing. In the early stages of planning, various themes were considered. The final theme was established in discussions with the Native people from the coast who participated in building the houses and in developing the different components of the exhibit. The exhibit affirms their life and cultural vitality in the present and explores their long and richly varied history.

The Native people of the Pacific Coast live on the islands, bays, and fjords of the sheltered waterway that runs along the west coast of Canada and southeast Alaska. Ancestral territories of coastal people also stretch inland along the rivers into the Coast Mountains.

The Pacific Coast is abundant in the resources that formed the basis of the traditional economy — salmon and eulachon in the rivers; herring, halibut, cod, seals, sea lions and whales in the open sea; seaweed and shellfish along the shore and on the rocks left visible by the receding tide; and, in the forests, berries, lupine roots, hemlock bark, and last, but extremely important, cedar, hemlock and yew.

When European explorers arrived in the 1770s, there were at least fifteen languages spoken on the coast, belonging to five distinct language families. Every region had its own languages, traditions, and distinctive identity.

The arrival of explorers, followed by fur traders, missionaries, the British Navy, and settlers, brought tragedy, opportunity and dilemmas to every family on the coast. The last years of the eighteenth century, and the nineteenth and twentieth centuries represent a period of innovation, change, resistance, loss, recovery, and ultimately, survival.

Facing page, *a fishing fleet, Alert Bay, 1980s*
(Photograph: V. Jensen)

Modern families on the coast, who deal every year with quotas on fishing boat licences, closures of the salmon fishery, the price of herring and the latest technology for immediate, on-board freezing of fish, also take time to smoke-dry dog salmon in October, to make eulachon oil in early spring — if eulachon runs in their territory — to dry halibut and herring roe, and to gather hemlock bark, rice root, soapberries and salal.

The real wealth of the coast, however, lies in certain privileges which exist now, and have existed for many generations. Inherited from ancestors, and publicly claimed and interpreted by each generation, these rights to the history of families and lineages, and to the demonstration of long-established relationships between human beings and supernatural beings, affirm the identity of their owners now as they did in the past. The crest figures on totem poles, the paintings on the houses, and the dances, songs, costumes and masks are all expressions of these inherited prerogatives.

In every generation, the Native people of the coast have negotiated the complexities of their own time while affirming the identity they have inherited from their ancestors. The Grand Hall exhibit explores that tradition.

The houses in the Grand Hall are arranged in the shape of a traditional village facing the sea. It is a symbolic village, however. Each house actually represents a diverse population occupying a large region of the coast.

The walk along the shoreline represents a walk from the southern to the northern coast — from the Coast Salish house past the Nuu-Chah-Nulth, Central Coast, Nuxalk and Haida houses to the Tsimshian. Along the shoreline are three environmental areas integral to the coast — a tidal pool, a grass-covered shore, and a river estuary. The forest, represented by a photograph reproduced on theatrical scrim, rises behind the houses and, between the Nuxalk and Haida houses, a forest clearing is visible.

Facing page, *the Haida village of Skidegate, Queen Charlotte Islands, 1982*
(Photograph: A. Laforet, Canadian Museum of Civilization)

Territories and Names

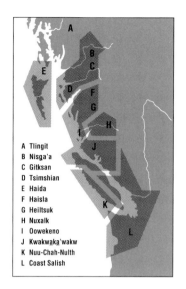

A Tlingit
B Nisga'a
C Gitksan
D Tsimshian
E Haida
F Haisla
G Heiltsuk
H Nuxalk
I   Oowekeno
J Kwakwaka'wakw
K Nuu-Chah-Nulth
L Coast Salish

FOR THE PURPOSES of the exhibit, each of the six houses in the Grand Hall represents many different groups of people who, although neighbours to one another in a large territory, are independent, have different names, and, in some cases, speak different languages.

In 1778, Captain Cook, one of the first European explorers, made the acquaintance of the Mowachaht people, one of approximately two dozen independently named groups of people living along the west coast of Vancouver Island. In an early conversation with their chief, Maquinna, Cook misunderstood their name as *Nootka*. Those who followed Cook from Europe applied the term Nootka to all the people of the west coast of Vancouver Island, and for the past two hundred years, the people themselves have been trying to correct this.

Since the arrival of the explorers, Native people on every part of the coast have contended with similar difficulties. In many cases, names were misunderstood or wrongly recorded. In all cases, single terms encompassed groups who were independent from one another, even if closely related through language or culture. *Coast Salish*, *Nootka*, and *Bella Coola* are all such terms. Many groups of people on the coast are now adopting names which are more closely based on tradition. *Kwakwaka'wakw* has replaced *Kwakiutl* as a term for all the Kwakwala-speaking groups. *Nuu-Chah-Nulth*, a modern term more acceptable than Nootka, expresses a contemporary political reality for the people of the west coast of Vancouver Island. Similarly, *Nuxalk* is used in preference to Bella Coola.

Above, *Peoples of the Coast*
This map shows the general location of territories. It is not intended to represent boundaries.

Facing page, *the Haida village of Skidegate, Queen Charlotte Islands, 1881*
(Photograph: Dosseter, courtesy of the American Museum of Natural History, 42264)

Alert Bay, ca. 1910
(National Archives of Canada, C 47366)

Houses and Totem Poles

IN THE PHILOSOPHY of the people of the coast, a house represents much more than shelter. It represents the family and the history of the family, all that the family has been and all it might be in the future.

The house was the place where families lived from generation to generation. The house anchored each family to its territory. Before the coming of the explorers, no one ever sold a house.

The people of the coast built their houses with a framework of cedar posts and beams. Walls were made of huge planks split from straight-grained cedar trees. The posts and beams, often carved to represent symbols of the family's history, carried the structure, while the planks of the walls could be removed at will. This is a principle of construction which did not enter the Western architectural tradition until recently.

The houses in the Grand Hall represent several architectural styles developed on the coast. Some of the houses are wholly traditional; others incorporate innovations which were made in the nineteenth century.

Totem poles associated with a house were the visible representation of a history of the family and the prerogatives it possessed. The term *totem pole* is recent, and has come to be used to refer to carvings which had different terms and functions in their original settings. Among the Haida, for example, there were house posts holding up the interior beams of houses, house frontal poles which also served as the doorway of the house, grave monuments and memorial columns erected in memory of a deceased chief, and interior poles which stood at the back of the houses of some high-ranking chiefs.

The poles carved on the Nass and Skeena rivers distilled the history of the lineage they represented, including the rights and territories owned by the lineage. The images on the pole, which were the crests of the lineage, represented a history recited at feasts by the lineage chief, who also inherited the right to serve as the custodian of that history.

Free-standing poles were rare on the central and southern coast until the late 1800s. In these regions, the large carvings were traditionally the posts supporting the roof beams of the houses, and house-front paintings displayed one or more of the family's principal crests.

The criteria for determining what images might be carved on a pole changed somewhat from region to region. Among the Gitksan of the Skeena River, it was rare to have the crests of two groups carved on a single pole. Among the Haida, grave monuments generally carried the crests of the deceased person, but house frontal poles could include crests of both the owner of the house and his wife, who always belonged to a different group (Swanton 1909: 122). Among the Coast Salish-speaking peoples of the southern coast, who defined relationships between human and supernatural beings somewhat differently from the northern peoples, carved house posts represented important ancestors, supernatural beings associated with the family's history, and events or privileges showing the spirit powers obtained by ancestors from supernatural beings (Kew 1980).

The figures on poles are combined in a way that is often difficult to decode several generations after the pole was made. A totem pole is a linear arrangement of carvings, but it is linear only in form. In conception it is a poetic array, with the figures chosen with a view to balance, form and connotation, as well as to explicit meaning. Consequently, while it is often possible to identify the figures on a pole through references to recorded myth, without knowing the particular history of the pole possessed by the family, it is impossible to "read" the pole.

With the exception of the Nuu-Chah-Nulth pole, for which a history has been provided by the Hesquiaht people, the descriptions given below for specific totem poles serve only to identify the pole in time and space. The history represented by each pole remains with the family, who has the prerogative to relate it.

The history represented by the crests on a pole involves not only the relationship between families and lineages, but also the relationship between human beings and animals. In the traditions of the coast, animals are seen as people, living in worlds only occasionally accessible to human beings, and possessing knowledge which human beings can acquire only through extraordinary experiences. Mountain goats, salmon, bears and other animals live in their own villages much as people do, and to visiting human beings they look like people. When they leave their own worlds and enter the human world, they arrive in their animal guises.

Traditional hunting and fishing constituted an exchange between animals and human beings. Animals allowed themselves to be killed for food; however, if their remains were properly handled, their death in the human world did not mean extinction, but a return to their own villages.

The relationship between human and animal beings is explored in oral traditions. There are many different traditions, with different purposes and characteristics. For generations, the tales of Raven, Mink and Blue Jay have been told and retold for instruction and entertainment. On the northern coast, Raven is a trickster, a wise man and a

*A house frame at the Kwakwa̱ka'wakw village
of Gwayasdums, 1900*
(Photograph: C.F. Newcombe, Royal British Columbia Museum, PN 241)

fool, who fashioned the Queen Charlotte Islands, shaped the features of the Skeena River country, and brought daylight to the world. On the central and southern coast, Mink and Blue Jay play the roles of trickster and innovator.

Trickster stories are available to everyone. In contrast, specific relationships between human families and animal and supernatural beings are described in the histories owned by each family and told formally at feasts. From the family history are derived not only the crests or emblems of family identity carved on totem poles and other kinds of property, but also names, songs, dances and the right to wear masks, headdresses, and dance costumes which evoke significant events in that particular history. These things embody the history of the family and also the identity and rank of the person who wears them. The ritual context in which these properties are displayed, and in which other prerogatives, such as membership in secret dance societies, are demonstrated, is a set of events which has come to be called the *potlatch*.

Potlatch, a Chinook jargon word meaning "to give" or "a gift," is often assumed to refer to something definite and uniform in the lives of the Native people of the coast. In fact, the events to which the term has been applied are different on every part of the coast. In general terms, however, a potlatch is an occasion at which guests, who are not part of the social group most clearly related to the hosts, are called to witness an event important to the host: the building of a house, the inheritance of a chief's title, the naming of children, the initiation of family members into a secret dancing society, the marriage of a child, or the erection of a totem pole. The term *potlatch* refers specifically to the distribution of gifts made by the host to the guests to acknowledge their role as honoured witnesses.

In each area of the coast, kinship relations determine succession to titles of rank, the passing of crests from one generation to the next, and the ownership of totem poles. Kinship systems differ from one part of the coast to another. Among the Tlingit, Haida and Tsimshian-speaking peoples of the northern coast, descent and inheritance are traced through the mother's line. Children belong automatically to their mother's group, and inherit crests, names and other properties from their mother's brother.

The Haida are divided into two groups: Ravens and Eagles. Eagles marry only Ravens; Ravens marry only Eagles. Each group has within it certain lineages. All Raven lineages share the Killerwhale crest and all Eagle lineages have Eagle as a crest, but each lineage also has certain crests derived from its own particular history.

The Tsimshian-speaking peoples have four groups, or phratries: Eagle, Frog/Raven, Wolf, and Blackfish or Killer Whale. Among the Gitksan of the Skeena River, the Fireweed group corresponds to the Blackfish.

On the central and southern coast, descent and inheritance are traced through both parents, although the Heiltsuk and Kwakwaka'wakw systems are different from the Nuu-Chah-Nulth and different again from the Coast Salish.

Construction of the Exhibit

Building the Houses

EACH OF THE SIX HOUSES was built and installed by a team of Native carvers from the region represented by the house. The houses were constructed in Vancouver, Masset and Alert Bay, with project coordination by the University of British Columbia Museum of Anthropology.

Many people worked on the houses. The published information on architectural styles of the coast yielded only the outline of what was needed for construction. Some architectural details were amply documented; others were entirely omitted from the record. The many photographs of nineteenth-century villages and houses provided

confirmation of some architectural conventions, but they also documented considerable variation. The final design draws on ethnographic records, historical photographs, the analysis of structural engineers, and the considerable help afforded to the teams by older Native people from the coast who shared their traditional knowledge generously.

The Coast Salish, Nuu-Chah-Nulth, Nuxalk and Tsimshian houses were built at two locations in Vancouver, on land provided by the Musqueam band. The Haida house was built outside Masset, and the Masset band provided assistance for some team members to travel to Hull to complete the construction. The Central Coast house was built in Alert Bay. Construction began in the late spring of 1988. In November 1988, members of each crew

From far left to right, *the Haida crew at work site on the Queen Charlotte Islands, 1988;*

The Coast Salish crew, Vancouver, 1988;

The Tsimshian crew, Vancouver, 1988;

The Nuxalk crew, Vancouver, 1988
(Photographs: B. McLennan)

travelled to Hull to assemble the houses. The members of the house-building crews are listed in the Credits.

The process of building the houses was a complicated one, with several stages: obtaining cedar logs of the required size and proportions; assembling tool kits; working out the large and small details of construction; and in some cases, bringing back into active use techniques which had not been employed in house construction for many decades.

Above left, *the Nuu-Chah-Nulth crew, Vancouver, 1988*
(Photograph: B. McLennan)

Above right, *Doug Cranmer before the Wakas house front, Alert Bay, 1988*
(Photograph: Ian Gregory)

Tools

THE CHAINSAW HAS BEEN PART of the Pacific Coast Native carpenter's tool kit since its invention. Through every stage of the construction and installation, traditional adzes were used side by side with chainsaws, each for a particular part of the work. Although D-adzes and elbow adzes have a longer history on the coast than chainsaws, they are all used for modern purposes.

It is customary for Native artists on the coast to make their own tools for fine work. Some of the people who worked on the houses had their own tools; others had to acquire them. Everyone needed the large-bladed adzes appropriate for working logs into finished beams.

Under the direction of Lyle Wilson, the crews of several houses made the tools they needed, using the shops at the Emily Carr School of Design in Vancouver. The adze blades were made of tempered steel, with the shape of the blade and the configuration of the edge determined by both tradition and the immediate requirement.

Preparing planks for the Haida house, Queen Charlotte Islands, 1988
(Photograph: B. McLennan)

Above, *adzing hand-split planks for the Coast Salish house, Vancouver, 1988*

Below, *adzing beams for the Nuu-Chah-Nulth house, Vancouver, 1988*

(Photographs: B. McLennan)

Lumber

THE HOUSES ARE MADE entirely of Western Red Cedar. Although the Pacific Coast is famous for cedar, and cedar constitutes a significant component of the British Columbia lumber industry, it is no longer an easy matter to obtain logs of the size appropriate for traditional houses. Some traditional house-building techniques, such as splitting cedar planks from logs, require logs of particularly straight grain, which are also increasingly difficult to find.

The massive beams of the Nuu-Chah-Nulth and Tsimshian houses required logs more than 12 metres (40 feet) in length, sound all the way through, and without twist. Finding such logs took time and patience, and there were several disappointing moments when logs of the right length and diameter were discovered to have rot at the centre.

Hand-split planks were used for the walls of the Coast Salish house and for the ceilings of all the houses. One hundred and fifty years ago, all houses on the coast were made of planks split from cedar logs, and the cedar growing in each region allowed for this. Now, it is possible to find cedar with sufficiently straight grain for splitting long planks only in a few old-growth forests. The wall planks for the Nuu-Chah-Nulth, Central Coast and Tsimshian houses were taken from the logs by means of an Alaska chain mill, and finished with adzing.

Lifting a finished beam into place on the Tsimshian house
in the Grand Hall, 1988
(Photograph: B. McLennan)

*Singing dedication songs for the Nuu-Chah-Nulth house
in the Grand Hall, November 1988*
(Photograph: B. McLennan)

Techniques

THE CONSTRUCTION OF THE HOUSES was an occasion for bringing back into use some techniques which were no longer common in house construction. These included the splitting of planks, the use of withes and poles to hold the walls of the Coast Salish and Nuu-Chah-Nulth houses together, the use of butterfly inserts to repair splits in planks, and the sewing together of planks to make a single broad surface, as on the Nuu-Chah-Nulth house front. The construction project also illuminated regional differences which were still important, but not often discussed, such as the differences in approach to adzing on the Coast Salish, Central Coast and Haida houses.

Although some artists had knowledge of the techniques of plank splitting, these techniques had not been used on a large scale on the southern coast in a long time. The Coast Salish house required split planks to make walls 12 metres (40 feet) in length and 6 metres (20 feet) in width. The planks were split with the traditional tool kit: wedges and mauls. The first plank was taken from the first log after several hours of careful planning and work. The last plank was split in a matter of minutes.

The ceiling of the Coast Salish house also represents the use of a traditional technique seldom seen now. The planks of the ceiling are lipped, so that when they overlap they provide a surface from which rain can quickly run off.

The horizontal planks of the walls of Coast Salish and Nuu-Chah-Nulth houses were traditionally held in place with cedar withes, long under-branches from the lower part of cedars growing in relatively open spaces. Gathered in spring, stripped of their bark, and twisted, they make an extremely tough binding material. While the technique was known in principle, there was considerable pessimism about the practicality of gathering and using withes in large quantities. The project was made more difficult by the fact that by the time the withes were required, the houses were already in Hull.

Like the plank splitting, the use of the withes proved to be somewhat easier than foreseen. Branches were gathered in quantity near Vancouver and on Vancouver Island, and brought to Hull in June 1989, just as the houses were nearing completion. Since the branches had to be thoroughly wet in order to be pliable enough to use, they were soaked in the river outside the Museum for several days. Several people worked through the last evenings before the Museum's opening day, stripping bark, twisting the branches and tying the finished withes between the

*Placing handprints around the doorway of the
Nuu-Chah-Nulth house, to make the rays of the sun,
June 1989*
(Photograph: B. McLennan)

planks. No one who worked on the project would under-estimate the effort involved, but the tying of withes is not a lost technique.

Withes were also used on the front of the Nuu-Chah-Nulth house to demonstrate the traditional technique of sewing planks together at the edges in order to make a broad flat surface which could then be painted for use as a house front. The Nuu-Chah-Nulth house front is made of six boards, 13 metres (40 feet) in length, the contours of the edges carefully matched so that they fit together. The withes are inserted along the edges, binding each plank to the plank below.

One of the planks on the Nuu-Chah-Nulth house front had a natural split, which the artist used to dem-onstrate a traditional technique for repair. Patches made of yew wood, shaped like butterfly bandages, were inserted into the wood, with the narrow point of the patch coin-ciding with the split in the plank.

The Exhibit

Coast Salish House

THE COAST SALISH ARE actually several related groups whose territories occupy much of the eastern coast of Vancouver Island and the mainland opposite. On the mainland, the territory stretches north to the Homathko watershed, east up the Fraser River beyond the present-day town of Yale, and south to the southern tip of Vancouver Island. People speaking Coast Salish languages are closely related to the Straits Salish people of the southern tip of Vancouver Island and the coast of Washington State.

There were two types of houses in Coast Salish villages, a long shed-roofed structure and a gabled house with a slightly pitched roof. Both types were constructed of heavy cedar logs holding up equally massive roof beams. The wide, hand-split cedar boards which formed the walls were set parallel with the ground between pairs of narrow poles and tied in place with twisted cedar branches. Traditional Coast Salish houses were very large, up to 30 metres (100 feet) in length and approximately 12 metres (40 feet) in width. Several related families lived in each house.

The house representing the Coast Salish in the exhibit is a smaller version of a house which stood near the present site of Nanaimo on Vancouver Island. Only three photographs have been found of this house, although, with its central doorway and massive carved figure and painting, it is somewhat unusual.

No record has been found of the exact significance of the carved figure in the doorway or the painting associated with it, but carved house posts and paintings inside Coast Salish houses often represent a supernatural being, frequently often known only to the person who had them made.

Neither the carving nor the painting associated with the original house are known to exist today. The painting was reproduced for the exhibit by Shane Point.

The Coast Salish village at Quamichan, ca. 1867
(Photograph: F. Dally, courtesy of the Royal British Columbia Museum, PN 1459)

Above, *Coast Salish house at Nanaimo,
showing potlatch platform, ca. 1900*
(Photograph: D.R. Judkins, courtesy of the
Royal British Columbia Museum, PN 1465)

Right, *Coast Salish house at Nanaimo, 1860s*
(Photograph: O.C. Hastings, National Archives of Canada, NAC 44197)

Tidal Pool

TIDAL POOLS ARE SMALL POOLS of water left in the crevices of rocks as the tide recedes. In the saltwater pool live the small creatures of the foreshore — feathery anemones, crabs, barnacles that open and close as they feed, and tiny green hermit crabs that make their homes in the black shells of turban snails. On the rocks are the shells of abalone, chitons, clams and mussels.

The people of the coast have relied on shellfish for thousands of years, and the huge shell middens, 3 to 5.5 metres (10 to 18 feet) deep, which mark the locations of old village sites bear witness to that fact. Mussel shells were used to make blades for knives and harpoons, but mussels and other shellfish were most important as sources of food. Some species were better in spring; others in the fall. It was possible, however, to gather shellfish all year long, except when winter storms brought exceptionally high tides. When the stores of salmon, halibut, berries and seal meat were exhausted, it was always possible to ward off famine with mussels, chitons and barnacles.

Today the gathering of shellfish is still important. Children are taught to recognize them, to know their names in the traditional language and to use them.

Nuu-Chah-Nulth House

NUU-CHAH-NULTH TERRITORY stretches from the northern part of western Vancouver Island south along the west coast to the western tip of the Olympic Peninsula in Washington State. Within this territory three closely related languages are spoken by the descendants of over twenty independent groups of people.

Nuu-Chah-Nulth houses could be as long as 30 metres (100 feet) and were built with cedar beams and hand-split boards according to the same principles as Coast Salish houses.

The Nuu-Chah-Nulth house in the Grand Hall represents a house which belonged to the head chief of the Tsesha'ath people who live near the present-day town of Port Alberni, at the head of Barkley Sound. The house stood in the 1800s. Although Nuu-Chah-Nulth houses were often set broadside to the beach, this house faced the beach. Below its large round doorway were ten round holes, representing ten moons. Above the entrance, two Thunderbirds faced each other, and above each Thunderbird was the figure of a Lightning Snake, the supernatural servant of the Thunderbird.

Above the Lightning Snakes were two supernatural Codfish, facing each other. The painting was created anew for the Nuu-Chah-Nulth house by Ron Hamilton, with the assistance of Lyle Wilson.

Nuu-Chah-Nulth house frame at Friendly Cove, 1874
(Photograph: R. Maynard, courtesy of the Royal British Columbia Museum,
PN 10508)

A Nuu-Chah-Nulth village, possibly Ahousat, 1860s (Photograph: F. Dally, courtesy of the Royal British Columbia Museum, PN 4649)

Nuu-Chah-Nulth pole
(Photograph: Hans Blohm,
Canadian Museum of Civilization)

Nuu-Chah-Nulth Pole

THIS POLE, A GIFT TO the Canadian Museum of Civilization from the Hesquiaht (Nuu-Chah-Nulth) people and the Royal British Columbia Museum on the occasion of the opening of its new building, was carved by Tim Paul, with the assistance of Kevin Cranmer. Art Thompson was commissioned to carve the headdress. The pole is approximately 8 metres (26 feet) high. The four main figures are derived from the history of the Hesquiaht people of central Vancouver Island. The Hesquiaht elders, through the Royal British Columbia Museum, have provided this explanation of the pole's figures:

TOP FIGURE
This represents a founding ancestor of the Hesquiaht, a chief named Ma-tla-ho-ah. He is posed in a dancing position and wears an elaborate headdress combining a mythical serpent with the visage of the first whiteman to come in contact with Hesquiaht people. The right to this headdress belongs to Chief Ben Andrew of Hesquiaht, a descendant of the original Ma-tla-ho-ah.

SECOND FIGURE
This represents a Thunderbird. Nuu-chah-nulth tradition states that when this mythic bird flaps its wings, it creates thunder and when it blinks its eyes, it causes lightning to flash. But this is a special Thunderbird belonging to the Hesquiaht people. It is said that it landed on a large flat rock in Hesquiaht harbour during a violent hail and lightning storm. The bird's body was obscured by a dark cloud so that only its talons were visible. The scratches which resulted from the bird's landing can still be seen on this rock today. Extending below each of the Thunderbird's

wings is a lightning serpent, the magical bolt the Thunderbird used to kill whales, which were its favorite prey.

THIRD FIGURE

Placed between the Thunderbird's wings is the third significant figure. This is a famed mythic sea mammal hunter renowned for his ability to catch whales, sea otters and seals. He holds a whaling harpoon in his hands. His story is as follows. His hunting territory was on the Estevan side of Hesquiaht. Every time he went seal hunting, he brought seals back to the village although they never numbered more than four for any given expedition.

His fellow villagers were amazed by his success. Unknown to them, he had discovered a sea cave where hair seal went to give birth to and raise their pups. The hero discovered a narrow shaft which led to the cave from atop a rocky cliff. He fashioned a rope from cedar branches and used this as a ladder to enter the sea cave. He would then club the number of seals required, haul them to the cliff top and then roll them down to the beach below.

The only person aware of his secret was his sister, who steered his canoe for him. She helped him load the carcasses prior to their return to the village. Feasting resulted with every delivery of seal meat but in time certain villagers grew concerned for they discovered earth in the mouths of the seals. How could this be associated with a sea creature, they wondered. Of course the dirt collected when the carcasses were rolled down the cliffside.

A rival hunter, whose territory lay to the Mowachaht side of Hesquiaht, secretly followed the hunter to his magic sea cave. Once the hero had descended via the cedar withe rope, the rival murdered the waiting girl and then hauled up the rope, thus trapping the hero in the cave. He languished in the cave for some time, sipping small quantities of salt water to keep alive. Before long he learned the language of the seals which still inhabited the cave. As he sat on a rock pinnacle above the high tide line, a female seal sang him a lullaby. The hunter admitted that all his people sought seals as food and warned them that once they had surfaced from a dive they were to look in all directions for approaching enemies. That is why today, when a seal surfaces, it scans the horizon in a complete circle.

Eventually the hunter felt a presence in the cave and heard a voice which whispered, "Your sister has been murdered." The intruder was a wolf who instructed the hunter to cling to its back and to keep his eyes closed no matter what befell him. The wolf then crept through the underwater passage which led to the open ocean. Several times the hero was bumped and scraped in the confined exit but he kept his eyes closed to avoid dying. Once outside the sea cave, the wolf released the hero and instructed him how to avenge his sister's death.

The hero returned to his village where he secured a magic crystal. He simply had to point it at an enemy or prey and they would die. The wolf told him that one night a whale would swim to the village shore. The hero was to show respect for the creature so that it would befriend him. Eventually the whale instructed him to paddle his rival out to sea and to entice the rival onto the whale's back. Once on the whale, the hero instructed his rival to cut into the blubber on the whale's back. Then the hero waved his crystal and the whale drifted far out to sea. "This is my revenge" he called to the stranded rival, "for it was you who killed my sister."

For nearly two months the unfortunate [man] drifted on the whale, almost out of sight of land; he cut a section from the whale's back and sat there in order not to be swept away. He nearly died of thirst and hunger. In time he came to know the whale and sensed that the whale was also a canoe. Finally he drifted to the north end of Vancouver Island and began to despair, certain that he was about to die. However he heard a voice say, "The Chief has given you permission to come ashore" and he soon found himself at Chickliset village. A man emerged from the whale and said, "Don't be afraid, I am a human although I will soon die. Enter the Chief's house and whenever you hear the house beams crack, go out to the beach, where a whale will drift in that you can claim. When I die, place my body (and thus my knowledge) in the Chief's box of treasures so that my power may remain."

FOURTH FIGURE
This represents the whale/canoe (note how the canoe forms pectoral fins) that took the rival out to sea. Note that his body is contained within the whale and that his mouth represents the whale's blowhole (Macnair 1989).

Central Coast House

ON THE CENTRAL COAST, north and east of the Nuu-Chah-Nulth, live the Kwakwaka'wakw, Heiltsuk, Owikeno and Haisla, politically distinct groups of people who speak different, though related, languages. Their territories, adjacent to one another, stretch from northern Vancouver Island to a point north of Kitimat. The façade of the house represents the house of Chief Wakas, a nineteenth-century chief who was descended from both the Owikeno and Nimpkish peoples.

The original house stood in Alert Bay (Yilis) from the early 1890s until at least the 1930s. Alert Bay was established on Cormorant Island off the northern coast of Vancouver Island by Nimpkish people whose home villages were located along the Nimpkish River on northern Vancouver Island.

In the early 1880s, a cannery was established at Alert Bay, and the community became a centre for commerce on the central part of the coast. Photographs of Yilis in the 1870s show a row of gabled houses with hand-split boards, and several of the houses have dramatic house-front paintings. The houses were still there in the 1890s, but owners were beginning to add façades of milled lumber to the fronts and to erect totem poles. The house in the Grand Hall represents Chief Wakas's house as it was in 1900.

When the carved pole was first erected in front of Wakas's house in the 1890s, the archway through the

The Wakas house, Alert Bay, ca. 1910
(Photograph: H.I. Smith, American Museum of Natural History, 46014)

bottom figure served as the entrance to the house. Shortly afterward, a beak was added by Kwakwa̱ka'wakw artist Dick Price. The top of the beak was the prow of a canoe, with the lower part specially made to complement it. Once the beak (large enough to admit a person) was added, the pole became a ceremonial entrance to the house. For everyday use, a narrow, rectangular doorway was cut through the façade beside the pole.

The façade of the house was originally white with a dark border. In 1899 or 1900, the Raven figure at the base of the pole was completed with the painting of tail feathers, wings and claws stretching across the façade and bringing the façade, the pole and the house itself together into a single representation of the history of Wakas's family.

The painting was made anew for the Grand Hall by Doug Cranmer, with the assistance of Bruce Alfred.

Wakas House-front Pole

CHIEF WAKAS' MOTHER was Nimpkish; his father was Owikeno, from the territory north of Alert Bay near Rivers Inlet. From his Owikeno ancestors, Wakas inherited a speaker's staff which represented the chief's authority and was used by a person speaking on behalf of a chief at a potlatch or other formal occasion. The carved figures on the staff are emblems of the chief's family history.

When he commissioned the entrance pole for his house, Chief Wakas had the carver re-create the figures on the speaker's staff except for one figure, a double-headed serpent, or *Sisiutl*, at the base of the staff. Inside the house, Wakas had a chief's seat with that Sisiutl figure.

The story of the pole concerns three brothers (the youngest named Wakas) who went into the forest in order to find out what had happened to their sister and other people of their village who had all disappeared. On the way, they met an elderly woman, rooted to the ground, who warned them that they would come to three houses. They would see a house with smoke like blood, which looked like a rainbow. This house belonged to Man-Eater-at-the-North-End-of-the-World. They would then come to a house with black smoke, belonging to the supernatural Grizzly, and next, to a house with white smoke, where the Mountain Goat lived. The woman gave them four items: a comb, a stone, a piece of cedar and some hair oil, to use if they needed to escape.

In the house with rainbow smoke — the home of Man-Eater-at-the-North-End-of-the-World — the brothers found their sister with a young boy, her son. The child was crying and would be comforted only when he was given blood to suck. The brothers looked around the house, and to their horror saw the bodies of their fellow villagers drying over the fire.

As the brothers left the house and began to run away, their sister called out to the Man-Eater, her husband. He pursued them through the forest as they ran back to their father's house. Each time the Man-Eater caught up with them, Wakas would use one of the gifts given by the old woman. The comb became a thicket; the stone, a mountain. The cedar stick became a log that moved back and forth across the Man-Eater's path, and the hair oil became a lake. As they slipped inside their house, Nenwaqawa, the boys' father, barred the door, but invited the Man-Eater to come back the next day with his wife and child. During the rest of that day, Nenwaqawa and his sons worked on a plan to kill the Man-Eater. They dug a pit in the back of their house, built a fire in it, put rocks in the fire to heat, and covered the pit, setting over it a chief's seat furnished with mats. Then they killed three dogs and removed their intestines, hiding the corpses so that the Man-Eater would not see them.

The next day, when the Man-Eater arrived with his wife and son, the three brothers lay just inside the door, covered with the dog's intestines. Thinking they were dead, the Man-Eater moved to eat them but was stopped by Nenwaqawa, who said it was the custom in that country to entertain guests with a story before the meal. He asked the Man-Eater and his family to sit on the chief's seat and he began to tell them a story. As he spoke, he tapped the ground with his speaker's staff in a rhythm which put them to sleep. When it was certain that they were all asleep, Nenwaqawa and his sons tipped the Man-Eater and his son into the hole, where they burned to death. Their ashes became mosquitoes.

The Man-Eater's wife, Nenwaqawa's daughter, was very upset when she woke up and realized her husband and son were dead. She explained that the Man-Eater had intended to marry her formally and to give Nenwaqawa his Man-Eater dance and his name, Man-Eater-at-the-North-End-of-the-World, as well as the privileges belonging to the other supernatural beings in his household.

As she spoke with her father and brothers, the Man-Eater's wife gradually became part of their family once again. She led them back to the Man-Eater's house and helped Nenwaqawa restore life to the bodies of the villagers stolen by the Man-Eater. Nenwaqawa and the people took the masks and treasures they found in the Man-Eater's house back to their own village. That same night, they held the first Man-Eater dance. This was the first winter ceremonial (after Boas 1921, II: 1222-1248).

Wakas's speaker's staff and the pole which commemorates it represent the speaker's staff used by Nenwaqawa as he told the story which lulled the Man-Eater to sleep. Several of the figures on the pole, Raven, Bear, Hohok and Wise-one (Nenwaqawa), were inspired by the story. Wolf, Killer Whale, and Thunderbird are also important in the winter ceremonial.

Chief Wakas's pole stood in Alert Bay until 1928, when it was purchased and moved to Stanley Park in Vancouver. In 1985, the pole was transferred to the Vancouver Museum. The Vancouver Museum, the Vancouver Board of Parks and Recreation, and the Canadian Museum of Civilization agreed in 1987 that the Canadian Museum of Civilization would borrow the pole for a period of thirty years.

A "new-generation" Wakas pole, commissioned by the Canadian Museum of Civilization and carved by Doug

Cranmer, with the assistance of Fah Ambers and Dickie Sumner, was erected in Stanley Park in May 1987. The original pole was restored for the Grand Hall exhibit by Doug Cranmer and Bruce Alfred in 1988. A new Raven's beak and a new Thunderbird were carved for the pole at this time, to replace earlier figures which were entirely worn away.

Inauguration of the new-generation Wakas pole in Stanley Park, Vancouver, May 1987
(Photograph: V. Jensen)

Village at Bella Coola, 1890s
(Courtesy of the American Museum of Natural History, 335773)

Nuxalk House

THE NUXALK, OR BELLA COOLA people, lived in at least forty-five villages located in a territory of mountains and sheltered fjords on the central coast. The word *Nuxalk* is derived from the term for the Bella Coola valley. The language spoken by the Nuxalk people is related to the languages spoken by the Coast Salish, the Straits Salish and other Salishan peoples of the interior of British Columbia.

The Nuxalk house in the Grand Hall is patterned after a house built in the village of Qwemqtc (Bella Coola) in the late 1800s, to represent Nusq'alst, a supernatural ancestor of Chief Clellamin. Nusq'alst came down to earth from Nusmat'a, the land above, at the beginning of the world. This was a time when the supernatural ancestors of many Nuxalk families came down from Nusmat'a and established homes and family lines on earth.

Nusq'alst first appeared as a man wearing a large hat, with living snakes around the brim. He settled in the Bella Coola valley and became a mountain, a place of immobilized power. As a mountain, Nusq'alst was a source of jadeite, the green stone used for adze blades.

The right to reproduce the peaks of the mountain on the roof of his house was a prerogative inherited by Clellamin from his ancestors. Among the peaks were carvings of deer and wolves, and two mountain goats looked down on passersby from windows in the gable of the central peak. On each peak was a carved wooden ball representing the rocks to which Nuxalk people tied their canoes during a flood which inundated the world in myth time. The peaks and gables were painted blue and white to represent the streaks of snow which can be seen even today on the mountain of Nusq'alst.

Above the door of the house was the figure of a man, a hammer in his hand. With the hammer, he pounded on a plank of maple, welcoming guests to the house when there was a feast. A sign placed above the sculpture after Clellamin's death in 1893 commemorates Clellamin's life.

The House of Nusq'alst combines both tradition and innovation. The people of the coast lived in houses that represented their supernatural ancestors and their family history. The construction of the houses embraced concepts of architecture and techniques of carpentry developed on the coast over centuries. At the same time, they were receptive to new ideas and techniques.

In 1885 several Nuxalk people travelled to Germany, where they stayed a number of months as performers in a show of traditional dances. Chief Clellamin's house incorporated European architectural influences and techniques in a house which, in keeping with Nuxalk tradition, is the living representation of the history of a family.

The house which stood in the 1890s no longer exists. The original sign over the door, the carved figure of the man with the hammer, and one of the mountain goats that looked from the gable windows are in the Museum's collection. As they would have been subject to harm from constant exposure to light in the outer part of the hall, they are represented by replicas on the reconstructed house. The other carvings associated with the original house apparently left Bella Coola before the 1920s and their present location is unknown. For the house in the Grand Hall, the two figures on either side of the doorway, and the wolf and deer on the roof were carved by the contemporary Nuxalk artist Glenn Tallio.

The original Clellamin house, 1913
(National Archives of Canada, NAC 95073)

Tallio Pole

THIS POLE, 7.6 METRES (25 feet) in height, originally served as the entrance to a house in the Nuxalk village of Tallio on South Bentinck Arm. It was later made into a grave monument and the disc was added to the top. The pole was purchased for the Museum in 1923.

The figures, from the top, are Eagle or Thunderbird; the Sun (represented by the disc); the Cannibal Giant (or Sharp Nose of the North), whose ashes were changed to mosquitoes when he was burned; the Beaver, an unidentified supernatural being; and a large face with a sharp nose and an open mouth which serves as the doorway.

The house at Tallio with its entrance pole in place, 1913
(Photograph: C.F. Newcombe, courtesy of the
Royal British Columbia Museum, PN 7200)

The village of Qwemqtc (Bella Coola), 1890s.
Qomoqua's house-entrance pole is at right.
(Photograph: I. Fougner, courtesy of the
Royal British Columbia Museum, PN 4575)

Chief Qomoqua's Pole

THIS POLE, WHICH IS 7.6 METRES (25 feet) high,
stood at the entrance of the house of Chief Qomoqua, two
doors down from Chief Clellamin's house.

The supernatural being Qomoqua was the ruler of the
undersea creatures who lived in his house. Qomoqua was a
powerful but elusive being. His face was kept blackened
and covered with down, and his features were never seen
because even when he appeared in front of people, he
turned away from those who might see him. Myths tell of
Nuxalk people who were caught in whirlpools and carried
down to Qomoqua's house. On occasion, his house rose to
the surface of the water, and to one ancestor of the Nuxalk
people, it appeared as a copper house with a loon totem
pole (McIlwraith 1948, I: 317). The walls of Qomoqua's
house were covered with paintings of sea creatures which
were painted and repainted as the tides rose and fell.

According to the notes of the collector, the figures
are, from the top, a supernatural chief with two cut-out
Killerwhale figures mounted as ears; the face of an Owl
who communicated the supernatural chief's wishes to
human beings; the Eagle; the human chief, Qomoqua,
who commissioned the pole; and the supernatural being
Qomoqua, who lived beneath the sea.

Haida House

THE HAIDA LIVE ON THE Queen Charlotte Islands (Haida Gwaii) and in the southern part of southeast Alaska. Masset and Skidegate, the principal contemporary communities on the Queen Charlotte Islands, are home to the descendants of people who lived in many villages all around the coast of the Queen Charlotte Islands.

The Haida house in the Grand Hall is a six-beam house, a style which became popular on the Queen Charlotte Islands in the nineteenth century. Haida houses had pitched roofs and a structure of hand-adzed timbers holding up the roof beams. The walls were constructed of boards set vertically and held at the top and bottom between timbers set parallel to the ground.

The six-beam house represents one of two styles. An older style had a structure of house posts holding up massive roof beams. In the nineteenth century the two styles co-existed in Haida villages.

"House Waiting for Property" Pole

ALTHOUGH THIS POLE SERVED as the entrance to a Raven lineage house in Haina (also spelled Xaina), on Maud Island near Skidegate, it originally stood in the village of Chaatl. There is some uncertainty about the name and lineage of the person who owned the house. According to one account, the owner was "He whose word is obeyed" of the lineage called the Pebble Town people. According to another, the owner was "One who moves the world as he walks" of Those Born at Hippa Island. The person from whom the pole was purchased belonged to Those Born at Hippa Island (MacDonald 1983: 65). The pole was collected in 1901 by the amateur ethnologist and collector C.F. Newcombe.

Both George MacDonald (1983: 65) and Marius Barbeau (1950, I: 288) have suggested an interpretation of the figures on this pole. The principal figures appear to be Eagle and Killer Whale. The central figures may relate to the story of an ancestor who travelled to the home of the Killer Whales under the sea in order to rescue the soul of his wife.

At the top of the pole are "Watchmen," small human figures wearing the dance hats often worn by chiefs at potlatches. A set of three figures often appears on Haida poles. They are said to have watched either for guests coming to a potlatch or for enemies, and to have alerted the chief accordingly. On the pole, the central Watchman wears a Killerwhale fin instead of a potlatch hat.

The original "House Waiting for Property" with its house-entrance pole, second from right, in the Haida village of Haina, 1888
(Photograph: R. Maynard, Canadian Museum of Civilization, CMC 20529)

Chief Wiah's House Post

WIAH WAS THE CHIEF of the Haida village of Masset in the mid-nineteenth century. His house, *Neiwans*, (Monster House), built around 1840, was famous for its great size and the depth of the platforms dug into the floor at the centre. The interior pole stood beside his private apartment (MacDonald 1983: 142).

Chief Wiah belonged to an Eagle lineage, and his house post, a Beaver with a sculpin carved on its belly, represents two of his principal crests. The stick which the Beaver holds in its mouth is inlaid with abalone shell. The interior pole, 5.5 metres (18 feet) in height, echoes a much taller memorial pole carved with the same figures. The taller pole stood outside Wiah's house.

The interior pole was purchased by C.F. Newcombe in 1902.

Chief Wiah's house post
(Photograph: Hans Blohm,
Canadian Museum
of Civilization)

Kayang Pole

THIS POLE, NEARLY 13 METRES (42 feet) in height, was associated with an Eagle lineage house in the Haida village of Kayang. The house was known as the "House that Wears a Tall Dancing Hat" (MacDonald 1983: 158).

The pole was exhibited at the World's Columbian Exposition in Chicago in 1893. After the exhibition, it became part of the original collection of the Field Museum of Natural History in Chicago, and was recorded as having been collected at Haina.

In 1931, the Field Museum sent the pole, along with several others, to the Century of Progress Exhibition in Chicago. It was subsequently sold to a Salvation Army boys' camp in Illinois and to two private collectors before it was purchased by the Canadian Museum of Civilization (then the National Museum of Man) in the early 1980s. During the period between its sale by the Field Museum and its purchase by this Museum, the pole lost five of the eight rings belonging to the top figure. These rings have been restored for this exhibit.

MacDonald (1983: 58) has described the figures on this pole as: chief with a tall dancing hat, embracing a small animal and joined to it by its tongue; Whale with human arms grasping its own fins; and Bear with a small raven in its mouth.

The Haida village of Kayang,
showing the Kayang pole at left, 1879
(Photograph: O.C. Hastings, courtesy of the
Royal British Columbia Museum, PN 10981)

The Haida village of Masset, showing the Fox Warren pole, third from right, in front of its original house, 1882
(Courtesy of the American Museum of Natural History, 32950)

Fox Warren Pole

THIS HAIDA POLE, approximately 12.3 metres (40 feet) in height, belonged to a house in Masset which was the property of a Raven lineage chief named "Things Roasted on a Fire." The figures on the pole, from the top, are three Watchmen; a figure in the centre with the tall hat representing Supernatural Snag; Supernatural Snag, shown as a standing figure with round teeth (to distinguish it from a bear); Supernatural Snag holding a frog; Grizzly Bear with a hunter; and Sea Wolf holding a whale (MacDonald 1983: 144).

In Haida cosmology, the snags that lie in wait under the water to catch and capsize canoes are supernatural beings. Grizzly Bear and the human figure represent the myth of the hunter who killed a bear and married the bear's wife. He supported the bear children born to this marriage, but in time returned to his human wife. Eventually both he and his bear children were killed in an attack on his village by the bear (MacDonald 1983: 9).

In 1882, Bertram Buxton, a wealthy Englishman travelling on the coast, purchased this pole and shipped it home to England, where it stood for many years at Fox Warren, the Buxton family estate near Weybridge. In 1978 the pole was purchased by the Museum and brought back to Canada.

While it was in England, the pole was covered with tar, intended as a preservative. In restoring the pole for exhibit in the Grand Hall, the Conservation Services Division of the Museum painstakingly removed the tar, revealing a surface on which could be seen not only the original sculptural lines of the figures, but also the fine adze work of the carver. On other poles of this period which have stood outside, the normal weathering process has worn away the original adze marks. The conservators also discovered fragments of very fine Haida cedar-bark matting, wadded together and placed under two wooden plugs used to fill holes in the wood.

The Fox Warren pole being restored by Conservation Services Division, Canadian Museum of Civilization

Estuary

THE SEA WAS IMPORTANT for fishing, but the rivers were vital. Four species of salmon — spring, sockeye, coho and dog — in addition to steelhead (which is technically a trout), spawn in the rivers from spring to fall.

In addition to weirs constructed of stakes and traps woven of branches and flexible strips of root, people used traps constructed of stone, which caught the salmon stranded by the receding tide.

Tsimshian House

THE COASTAL WATERWAYS opposite to and north of the Queen Charlotte Islands, the waterways just north of Haisla territory and the Nass and Skeena river valleys, and the adjacent lands constitute a huge region which is home to four different peoples: the Nisga'a of the Nass River and the adjacent coast; the Gitksan of the upper Skeena River and its tributaries; the Coast Tsimshian of Port Simpson and the coastal waterways to the south, including the initial portion of the Skeena River; and the Southern Tsimshian. At least three languages are known: Coast Tsimshian, Nass-Gitksan and Southern Tsimshian.

The Tsimshian house represents a style of house which stood in Tsimshian villages in the mid-1800s. In construction, it is similar to Haida houses, with a structure of massive cedar posts and beams and removable vertical wall boards, set into grooved timbers top and bottom. The houses of high-ranking people among both the Tsimshian and Haida had central fire pits, with broad steps leading down from the main floor. The steps were wide enough to accommodate meal preparation and other domestic activities. The Tsimshian house will eventually include such a pit.

The painting on the front of the house is a re-construction of a screen used in the Coast Tsimshian village of Port Simpson in the mid-1800s. The central figure represents a bear, and the flanking figures represent wolves.

The house-front painting first found its way into the University of British Columbia Museum of Anthropology as a set of boards, recorded in the catalogue as having been found in Port Simpson in waterlogged condition by a

Fort Simpson (later Port Simpson), 1873
(Photograph: Horetzky, courtesy of the
Provincial Archives of British Columbia, 10719)

medical missionary, Dr. Raley. There was no indication of the original owner of the boards or of their original purpose.

As infrared photography revealed the design on the boards, it became evident that these boards were part of what had been a huge screen, with a large central figure and two flanking figures. The absence of signs of severe weathering of the paint and the nature of the accumulated grime on the surface indicated that it had served as an interior screen, rather than as a house-front painting. It was also evident that the design was incomplete. The boards Raley had collected were only part of the original screen.

The project to re-create the complete design was carried out under the direction of Bill McLennan at the University of British Columbia Museum of Anthropology, with assistance from the Canada Council and the Canadian Museum of Civilization.

The area of the Grand Hall exhibit occupied by the Tsimshian house represents four peoples: the Coast Tsimshian, the Nisga'a, the Gitksan and the Southern Tsimshian. The totem poles erected near the house, the Kwahsuh pole, the Bear's Den pole, and the White Squirrel, are from Nisga'a and Gitksan villages on the Nass and Skeena rivers.

Kwahsuh Pole

THIS POLE, 14 METRES (45 feet) in height, represents Li'ins, chief of a leading Nisga'a Wolf lineage. It was erected around 1870 by Kwahsuh (Matthew Nass), head chief of the Neesles'yaes Wolf phratry at the Nass River village of Angidah. The name of the pole is "Thl'ameen," meaning "Wide Base" or "Wide Bottom." It was purchased by Marius Barbeau and Art Price in 1947.

The figures on the pole, from the top, are Grizzly Bear or Grizzly Bear Cub; a small grave box placed on Cane-of-the-Sky in memory of another Kwahsuh, who had succeeded to the title but died in infancy; a grave box placed in memory of Hlabeks, another important chief in the household of Kwahsuh; Wolf (a principal crest) on top of this box; a face representing another crest, "Split Person"; Chief of the Wolves holding Grizzly Bear's copper in his teeth; and Grizzly Bear, pointing downward and holding a salmon and two bear cubs with another cub on her chest, representing "All Children of the Grizzly Bear," and faces carved in the paws of the bear mother, representing "People of the Smokehole."

Although there was later some uncertainty about the identity of the carver, Barbeau recorded that the owner of the pole had said it was carved by Gwans and Weesaiks, both members of the Gispewudwade (Killer Whale) phratry of the village of Gitwinsilk (Barbeau 1950, I: 232).

The two boxes on the pole, apparently lost when the pole was collected, have been replaced for the exhibit with the help of archival photographs of the pole in its original village.

The Kwahsuh pole
(Photograph: Hans Blohm, Canadian Museum of Civilization)

Bear's Den Pole

THIS POLE, CALLED "BEAR'S DEN," stood in the Nass River village of Gwunahaw. It was carved by Weeshaiks, a member of the Fireweed phratry. Barbeau recorded two possible dates, 1892 and 1910. Weeshaiks was assisted by two other carvers, Neesqawrhse of the Fireweed phratry, and Leonard Douglas, a member of the Wolf phratry of Kwahsuh.

The pole was erected by 'Arhtimenazek, and the figures are related to the history of his lineage. The small animal in the round hole is Bear Cub (Barbeau 1950, I: 237).

The Bear's Den pole was purchased by Marius Barbeau in 1929, and sold to the Museum of the American Indian in New York City. It was purchased by the National Museum of Man (now called the Canadian Museum of Civilization) in 1977.

The Bear's Den pole, 1927
(Photograph: C.M. Barbeau, Canadian Museum of Civilization, CMC 69645)

White Squirrel

THE WHITE SQUIRREL was a lone figure sitting on top of the last of twenty-four poles that stood along the shore of the Nass River at Gitlakdamiks. It belonged to Hrtsiyae, member of an Eagle lineage at Gitlakdamiks, and commemorated Qastu'in, one of his Eagle kinsmen. The White Squirrel was carved during the 1870s by 'Niesyawk, head of a Wolf lineage in Gitlakdamiks. 'Niesyawk, an elderly man when Barbeau visited the Nass River in 1927, was assisted by Witiyaetk, member of a Fireweed phratry at the Skeena River village of Gitsegyukla. Barbeau purchased the White Squirrel for the Museum in 1929. The pole and box on which it sits in the Grand Hall were newly made for the exhibit.

In connection with another pole, the Dog Salmon pole from the Gitksan village of Kitwanga on the Skeena River, Harlan I. Smith recorded a legend concerning the White Squirrel:

> Once upon a time the Squirrels, led by the White Squirrel (their chief), warred on the Indians of the Skeena River, giving them no peace by day or by night. They so harassed the Indians that at last they overawed them. When [sic] Duwallis (Tewalas), who was not only a noted fisherman, but also a renowned warrior, came forward and fought the White Squirrel single-handed. He choked him to death, and, by so doing, brought so much dismay to all the Squirrels that it ended the war. (Smith 1926, pole 10)

According to Barbeau (1929: 139), the Squirrel crest was used only by the families of Tewalas at Kitwanga and

The White Squirrel, 1972
(Photograph: T. Rundle and B. Lebeau, Canadian Museum of Civilization, CMC 72-2334)

Qowq at Gitlakdamiks. The encounter of the family of Tewalas with the giant Squirrels occurred while the family was camped at a salmon fishery on the Nass River.

Haida Canoe

THE HAIDA CANOE was built by Alfred and Robert Davidson near their home at Masset on the northern Queen Charlotte Islands. The canoe was commissioned for the Seattle Exposition of 1908, and, when finished, was taken across the strait to Prince Rupert. Although it was equipped with masts and sails, the canoe was towed behind a steamer. During the voyage, a storm came up, and the tow cable was severed. The steamer captain, believing that the canoe and its passengers were lost, went on to Prince Rupert. When he arrived, he found the canoe already tied to the dock (Dalziell 1968: 41).

The arrangement with the Seattle purchaser was never completed. The canoe was returned to the Queen Charlotte Islands, where it remained until its purchase by the Museum in 1910.

A northern canoe, southeast Alaska.
Sails were in common use during the late nineteenth century.
(Photograph: Blankenberg, courtesy of the
Royal British Columbia Museum, PN 9152)

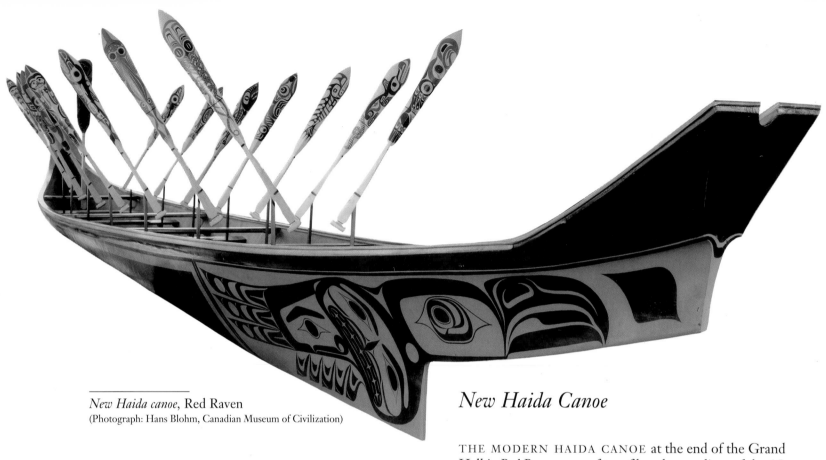

New Haida canoe, Red Raven
(Photograph: Hans Blohm, Canadian Museum of Civilization)

New Haida Canoe

THE MODERN HAIDA CANOE at the end of the Grand Hall is *Red Raven*, one of two fibreglass replicas of the 15-metre (50-foot) cedar canoe made in 1986 by Haida artist Bill Reid. The original canoe, *Lootas* (Wave-Eater), was made at Skidegate on the Queen Charlotte Islands and exhibited at Expo '86. In the same year, a crew of Haida people paddled *Lootas* from Vancouver to the Queen Charlotte Islands.

The two fibreglass canoes, *Red Raven* and *Black Eagle*, were made in Vancouver in 1988 for the opening of the Canadian Museum of Civilization. The canoes and their paddles were painted by Bill Reid.

Raven Bringing Light to the World
(Photograph: Harry Foster,
Canadian Museum of Civilization, K89-804)

Raven Bringing Light to the World

RAVEN BRINGING LIGHT TO THE WORLD, a sculpture
in gold on bronze by contemporary Haida artist Robert
Davidson, represents the legend of Raven, trickster and
transformer, who stole the box of light and let it spill over
the world.

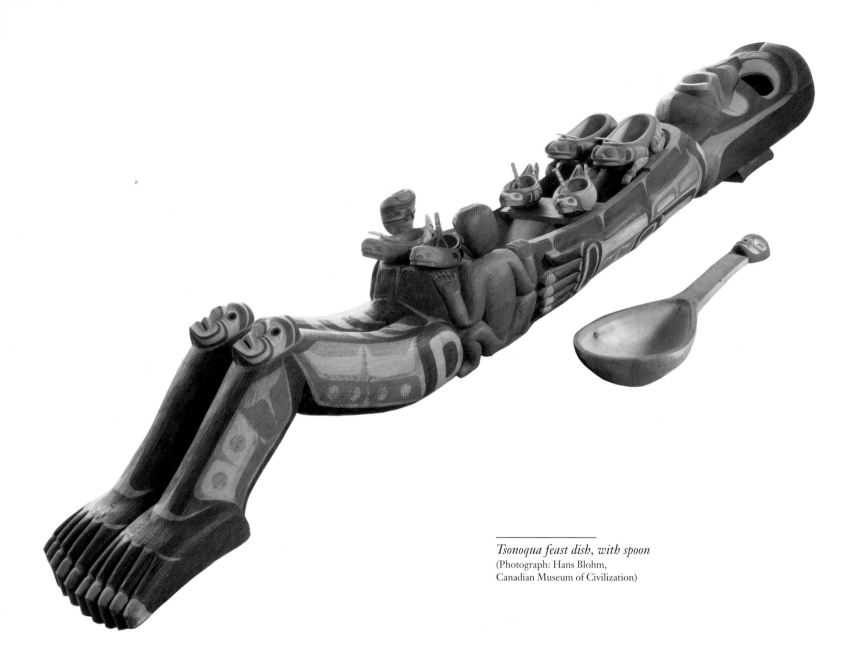

Tsonoqua feast dish, with spoon
(Photograph: Hans Blohm,
Canadian Museum of Civilization)

Tsonoqua Feast Dish

ABOUT 8 METRES (27 feet) long, the Tsonoqua feast dish in the Grand Hall is a contemporary work which rivals in size the large, traditional feast dishes. Many Kwakwaka'wakw stories tell of Tsonoqua, a supernatural woman who lived in the depths of the forest. Huge, shambling, and half-blind, with a basket on her back to hold the children she sought to capture, she was a figure to be feared. At the same time, she was a symbol of riches and wealth.

The wealth of the coast was evident in the abundant food it offered. The salmon, halibut, seal meat, venison, eulachon oil, lupine roots, berries and hemlock bark gathered through the seasons were eaten not only at daily meals but also at feasts. The food at feasts was often placed in a large dish carved in the form of an animal or supernatural being, and was served to guests in smaller dishes shaped like seals, wolves or sea otters.

The abdomen of the Tsonoqua in the Grand Hall is the main part of the feast dish, while the face can be removed to reveal another dish. Associated with the feast dish are six small bowls, in the form of red snappers, seals and frogs, which, when the dish is completely assembled, rest on the knees and other parts of Tsonoqua's body. Food is transferred from the feast dish to the bowls with a huge ladle.

The Tsonoqua feast dish was made for the Canadian Museum of Civilization by Kwakwaka'wakw artist Calvin Hunt.

Scrim

THE DENSE FOREST of the Pacific Coast is represented in the Grand Hall by an image reproduced on scrim, an open-meshed cloth often used in theatrical scenery. The scrim is approximately 76 metres (260 feet) long, and runs the full length of the village behind the houses. There are actually two scrims, each displaying an image of the forest and placed one behind the other for a three-dimensional effect.

The image for the scrim was produced from photographs taken on the coast during the summer of 1988. Five sites were surveyed; the site that was chosen to be photographed is on Vancouver Island.

To create the entire image, ten prints, measuring 50 by 69 centimetres (20 by 24 inches), were mounted in a mosaic format approximately 5 metres (16 feet) in length. Overlap between the images was corrected and balanced by an illustrator, and the tree-top mist added through airbrushing. The completed image was photographed in a series of 20 by 25 centimetre (8 by 10 inch) transparencies.

In the production stage, the image was applied to 9 by 9 metre (30 by 30 foot) sections of theatrical scrim by a California company using a computer-controlled process.

Inside the Houses

EXHIBITS FOR THE INTERIOR of each house in the Grand Hall are being developed in cooperation with the Native people of the region concerned. Two of these exhibits can be seen in the Central Coast and Nuxalk houses. Short-term exhibits showing selections from the collection may be seen in the other houses while the cooperative exhibits are under development.

Kwakw<u>a</u>ka'wakw Exhibit

THE THEME OF THE EXHIBIT in the Central Coast house is the Kwakwaka'wakw potlatch. The exhibit represents three time periods: 1890-1910, when the original house was standing in Alert Bay and when many of the masks and feast dishes now in the Museum's collection were made and used; the 1930s, when the potlatch was actively suppressed by law but maintained quietly by families; and the present day.

In the first section, feast dishes, a carved figure showing the importance of a chief, and other objects associated with the turn-of-the-century potlatch are presented. These include bolts of cloth, brass oar locks, lanterns, sacks of flour, Hudson's Bay blankets, canoes and other goods given to guests at a potlatch at this time. Opposite are masks from the same period, shown in seclusion behind a dance screen made of wooden planks in the old style. The dance screen is modern, although the design has been used by a particular family for several generations. If still in use, masks are shown only when they are worn by dancers. At other times they are kept in seclusion, out of respect for their power. In keeping with this custom, the masks in the exhibit are shown behind the screen.

The 1930s section shows a room in the house of a Kwakwaka'wakw family as it was in 1937. The house post in the room stood in the family's home for many years. Carved in 1925 by Kwakwaka'wakw artist Charlie James, it was made in memory of a house post on Village Island which had been destroyed in a fire. The house post was purchased by the Museum in 1977.

In the third section, a six-projector slide show presents the history and contemporary meaning of the potlatch. The final section shows potlatch gifts of the kind given to guests in the 1990s. The principles are the same as they were a century ago: Suitable gifts are food, baskets and other containers, and textiles, such as blankets and tea towels. The form of the gifts is contemporary.

Two house posts stand at the back of this house. They originally stood as interior posts in the house of Chief George of Nahwitti. Both have Grizzly Bear as the principal figure. On one, the bear holds a human figure, the bear's feet resting on a second human figure; on the other the bear also holds a human figure, but the bear's knees are bent over the figure of a Raven.

Facing page, *interior of the Central Coast House showing the 1930s display*
(Photograph: Hans Blohm, Canadian Museum of Civilization)

Nuxalk Exhibit

THE EXHIBIT IN THE NUXALK house explores the meaning of family histories to the Nuxalk people — both in the past and present day. Developed in cooperation with members of the Nuxalk community at Bella Coola, the exhibit presents the masks which embody the rights and privileges inherited by contemporary Nuxalk people from their ancestors.

Most of the Nuxalk masks were collected in the 1920s. They derive their meaning, however, from the stories which connect families with supernatural ancestors. That meaning remains important today.

At the rear of the house stands a large carving, shown in turn-of-the-century dress and a modified potlatch hat. The figure is 3 metres (9 feet, 3 inches) high, with out-stretched arms 7 metres (23 feet) in length. Originally this figure stood in the house of a Nuxalk man, Captain Schooner. His house was a few doors away from the original Clellamin house. The figure stood against the rear wall of the house, its outstretched arms appearing to hold up the roof beams. It was purchased by Harlan I. Smith for the Museum in 1920.

Facing page, *interior of the Nuxalk House,*
with exhibit of Nuxalk headdresses and masks
(Photograph: Hans Blohm, Canadian Museum of Civilization)

Along the Windows

T HE TOTEM POLES along the windows in the
Grand Hall, across from the village, are part of the
Museum's collection of traditional poles. They are
from several different villages on the coast, and were collected by the Museum at various times between 1905 and
the present day.

Standing-on-the-Beach

ALTHOUGH THIS FIGURE was called "Standing-on-the-
Beach" *(te'isimi)*, it stood in the centre of a house built by a
Nuu-Chah-Nulth man, Nawek', who was also known as
Tom Sayachapis. Nawek' had the house built on the
occasion of his daughter's coming into womanhood.
Carved by Klapinamix, the figure held up the central beam
of the house and faced the rear wall, so that people sitting
in the place of honour at the rear of the house could see it.
Standing-on-the-Beach represents two hereditary privileges of a Nuu-Chah-Nulth family combined in a single
figure. The large human-like figure represents the Creator
of the Tsesha'ath people, whose village is at the present site
of Port Alberni on Vancouver Island. The oval carving in
his hands represents a privilege inherited by the family and
used at potlatches.

The figure, Standing-on-the-Beach, and the "potlatch
handle" game were distinct privileges which Nawek'
inherited from different parts of his family. In his house,
they were combined in a single carved figure.

At certain potlatches, the carving was taken from the
hands of Standing-on-the-Beach and thrown into the
audience. The person who caught it and wrested it free
from the other people won a prize. There were songs
associated with this game; the right to sing them and the
right to the game itself were inherited. Nawek' inherited
this privilege through his father's mother, who received it
as part of her dowry.

Standing-on-the-Beach represents a post which stood
in a house discovered by the supernatural ancestor of the

Tsesha'ath people when he himself was first created. As well as representing the Creator, it is also intended to bring to mind the first days when the Tsesha'ath people came into being. The black and red paint on the face is the face paint worn by the ancestor, and was worn by him when he gave feasts (Sapir, no date).

Standing-on-the-Beach
(Canadian Museum of Civilization, J-18730-1)

Nahwitti House Posts

THESE CARVED POSTS are associated with a house in the Kwakw<u>aka</u>'wakw village of Nahwitti at the north end of Vancouver Island. They were purchased by C.F. Newcombe in 1899.

The first is an interior post used to support one end of a roof beam. The figure is Tsonoqua, Wild Woman of the Woods, and a symbol of wealth. The second post is the figure of a man.

Left, *the Nahwitti house post, with the figure of Tsonoqua*

Right, *the Nahwitti house-entrance figure*

(Photographs: Hans Blohm, Canadian Museum of Civilization)

Sisiutl House Posts

THESE POSTS, CONSISTING of three upright figures supporting a massive carving of Sisiutl, a supernatural serpent, were erected around 1884 at the Kwakwaka'wakw village of Dzawadi in Knight Inlet. In the early 1880s, Dzawadi was a village with houses, fishing camp shelters and some freestanding carved poles. According to the collector's documentation, the house posts were erected at the annual gathering of people at Knight Inlet for the eulachon fishing in early spring.

The house for which the posts were intended was never built. The posts stood at Dzawadi until 1913, when they were purchased by Victoria politician James Dunsmuir and erected on his estate at Esquimalt, near Victoria. In 1938, they were bought by collector George Heye for the Museum of the American Indian in New York, where they remained until they were purchased in 1975 by the National Museum of Man (now called the Canadian Museum of Civilization).

The upright figures consist of two humans flanking a bird. The Sisiutl figure consists of the two heads of the supernatural serpent, with a human face in the centre. The three posts were intended as supports for the roof beams, while the Sisiutl carving was intended to define the roof line above the door of the house.

The height of the Sisiutl house posts is 3.65 metres (12 feet), and their length is approximately 13 metres (41 feet, 9 inches).

The house posts and Sisiutl carving at Dzawadi, 1913, after a grass fire which partially burned them
(Photograph: C.F. Newcombe, courtesy of the Royal British Columbia Museum, PN 6893)

Cape Mudge House Posts

THESE TWO HOUSE POSTS, each carved with figures of Eagle and Beaver, support a plain cross beam. The birds originally had wings, which have not survived.

These posts were associated with a house in the Kwakwa̱ka'wakw village of Cape Mudge on Quadra Island. They were purchased for the Museum by Harlan I. Smith in 1929.

Tanu Pole

THIS INTERIOR POLE stood at the centre of the back wall of "Easy to Enter" House, owned by Kwagians, a member of an Eagle lineage in the Haida village of Tanu. The pole actually belonged to Kwagians's wife, and it portrays the crests of the family of the Chief at Skedans. At the base is Grizzly Bear, with a Sea Grizzly at the top. A long, carved spiral stick, associated with the house post and reported to have been stuck between the two figures, was used as a staff by the chief during speeches at feasts (MacDonald 1983: 97). The pole and staff were purchased by C.F. Newcombe in 1902, and sent to the Field Museum of Natural History in Chicago.

In 1931 the Tanu pole and three other Haida poles were lent to the Century of Progress exhibition in Chicago. The poles were not returned to the Field Museum, but were sold in 1933 to the Salvation Army Boys' Camp at Lake Antioch, Illinois. They were subsequently bought by collectors in California and Maine, and were finally purchased in 1982 by the National Museum of Man (now called the Canadian Museum of Civilization).

When the Tanu pole was in private hands, it was extensively repainted in colours much brighter and more various than the sober black, red, and blue which the Haida used to highlight features of monumental carving. The weathered cedar absorbed a considerable amount of the new paint. Since the pole was purchased by the Museum, members of the Conservation Services Division staff have taken pains to identify original paint (on eyebrows, eye pupils, lips and nose) and to remove layers of added paint.

The Tanu pole is approximately 5.5 metres (17 feet, 11 inches) high.

Facing page, *the house posts at Cape Mudge, 1929*
(Photograph: H.I. Smith, Canadian Museum of Civilization, CMC 72808)

Right, *the Tanu interior pole* in situ, *1901*
(Photograph: C.F. Newcombe, Royal British Columbia Museum, PN 105)

Dog Salmon Pole

THE DOG SALMON POLE stood at the Gitksan village of Gitwangak (Kitwanga). It was erected in honour of Tewalas, a high-ranking member of the Eagle (Laxskik) phratry. Like other important names on the coast, the name Tewalas is inherited from generation to generation.

The theme of the carving is the relationship between a Tewalas who was a renowned warrior and accomplished fisherman, and the Dog Salmon. In an account recorded by Harlan I. Smith in 1926, the Dog Salmon pole represents the seizure of Tewalas by the Dog Salmon. Tewalas speared a giant dog salmon, and was dragged out of his canoe and taken down to the village of the Dog Salmon under the Skeena River. He spent two years there and then returned to Gitwangak, knowing the Dog Salmon so well that he could catch them whenever he wanted. He became rich and powerful, but died in a battle with the people of Kitselas, who split his body in half.

MacDonald (1984: 77-78) identified the five figures on the pole as Person-with-the-fish-spear, standing on the tail of the Dog Salmon, with the Salmon's tail emerging from his head; Dog Salmon; Split-person, holding the fin of a second dog salmon with his head in the mouth of the first salmon; Dog Salmon with two dorsal fins; and Split-person in the mouth of the second salmon.

Barbeau (1929: 138-9) recorded that the Dog Salmon crest originated with a Kitselas family related to the family of Tewalas. By showing particular respect for dried salmon,

The Dog Salmon pole (far left) at Gitwangak
(Photograph: H.I. Smith, 1915, Canadian Museum of Civilization, CMC 34595)

a young man had cured the Salmon Chief of an illness. The salmon, who were grateful, appeared to him as human beings and took him in their canoe to their own home. In their village were three large houses belonging to the Dog Salmon, the Steelhead Salmon and the Spring Salmon. The salmon lived in this village as human beings.

When it was time for the salmon run, they gave the young man a salmon cloak. He changed into a salmon and swam upriver until he came to his village. His uncle caught him, thinking he was a giant salmon, but soon discovered who the giant fish really was. The Dog Salmon became the crest of the family.

The Dog Salmon pole stood on its original site beside the river at Gitwangak until 1926, when it was restored under a programme carried out jointly by the National Museum of Canada (a forerunner of the Canadian Museum of Civilization) and the Canadian National Railways. At that time, it was moved a few metres from its original position. In 1936, when the pole was once again endangered by the erosion of the river bank, it was restored by the people of Gitwangak, and moved along with other poles to a point 200 metres to the north. By 1961 the pole was lying on the ground. In 1970 it was purchased by the National Museum of Man. A mould was made of the original pole, with the consent of the owner and the cooperation of the Skeena Totem Pole Preservation Society. A fibreglass replica was made of the original pole and erected at Gitwangak.

The height of the Dog Salmon pole is 10.9 metres (35 feet, 11 inches).

Rainbow Pole

NOTE: The Rainbow pole, Lightning House pole and the Rock Slide House pole, described on the following pages, were brought back to Canada from the United States by the Canadian Museum of Civilization between 1977 and 1982. All require considerable conservation treatment. Once the conservation work is completed, these poles will be erected in the Grand Hall.

THE RAINBOW POLE stood at Gwunahaw, a Nass River village near the village of Gitwinksilk. It belonged to Gwaneks and 'Weelarhae of the Fireweed phratry. It was known on the Nass River as *Niqanskyi*, meaning "lies over the top." The figures, from the top, are Niqanskyi, holding the Rainbow *(marhe)*, a crest of the phratry; the Blackfish or Killer Whale *('naerhl)*; one-legged being *(negut-ligirhna'ts)*; sun *(hlawqs)*; an unidentified figure; Grizzly-Bear-of-the-Sea *(mediegemdzawey'aks)*.

The pole was raised to commemorate a person who had held the name Gwaneks in an earlier generation. The date the pole was raised is uncertain. Both 1892 and 1911 have been suggested. The identity of the carver is also uncertain. Some of Barbeau's consultants believed it was carved by Qaderh, a member of the house of Kyarhk, of the Wolf phratry of the Nass River village of Gitlakdamiks, while others believed the carver was Nigwen (Bryan Peel), who was also from Gitlakdamiks (Barbeau 1950, II: 438).

The village of Gwunahaw was deserted by 1929, although people were living at the nearby village of Gitwinksilhk. The people whom Barbeau consulted remembered that there had been a second pole, exactly the same as the Rainbow pole, which had stood on the other side of the canyon. This pole burned down in 1892 in a fire which destroyed the village and most of the poles.

The Rainbow pole, which is 10.42 metres (approximately 34 feet) high, was purchased by Marius Barbeau in 1929 for the Museum of the American Indian in New York. It stood for a number of years outside the Museum of the American Indian Annex in the Bronx. It was purchased in 1977 by the National Museum of Man (now called the Canadian Museum of Civilization).

The Rainbow pole, 1927
(Photograph: C.M. Barbeau, Canadian Museum of Civilization, CMC 69639)

Lightning House Pole

THIS HOUSE ENTRANCE POLE, like the "House Waiting for Property" pole by the Haida house, was originally erected at the Haida village of Cha'atl, but was moved in the latter part of the nineteenth century to the village of Haina (now called New Gold Harbour) on Maud Island, near Skidegate. It was the entrance to the Ts'amti (Lightning) House, which belonged to the town chief, Ganai, a member of the Pebble Town Eagle lineage.

The figures, from the top, are Raven; a myth figure wearing a dance hat; Raven with a downturned beak; a myth figure; and Thunderbird (MacDonald 1983: 65). The pole was purchased in 1902 by C.F. Newcombe for the Field Museum of Natural History, and is 13.7 metres (45 feet) high.

The Lightning House pole in the Haida village of Haina, 1880s
(Courtesy of the Field Museum of Natural History, Chicago, neg. A17460)

Rock Slide House Pole

THIS HAIDA POLE belonged to Rock Slide House, which was erected in the late 1800s in the village of Cumshewa. This house replaced an earlier one on the same site, "House that Makes a Great Noise." The figures, from the bottom, are Grizzly Bear; Killer Whale with protruding dorsal fin and a woman clinging to its tail; Cormorant; and three Watchmen (MacDonald 1983: 74).

The pole, 12.2 metres (40 feet) in height, was originally purchased in 1901 by C.F. Newcombe for the Field Museum of Natural History.

The Rock Slide House pole at the Haida village of Cumshewa
(Courtesy of the Field Museum of Natural History, Chicago, neg. A16314)

Conclusion

THE GRAND HALL EXHIBIT was originally planned as a glimpse into the past, with the houses aged to look like houses from the nineteenth century. As the exhibit developed, it became clear that this approach did not accommodate certain concepts of vital importance on the coast.

During the initial consultation with the communities about the houses and house-front paintings, the concept of house and the ownership of the prerogatives represented by the house-front paintings were affirmed to be as vital in the present generation as they had been in the past. The artists who built the houses clarified and extended this principle. In their view, the houses were not replicas, but modern houses built in architectural styles which had been used in the past but belonged to the Native people of the coast in all generations. From this perspective, there was no need to age the wood. Accordingly, the houses stand in the hall as they were built.

On the coast, the relationship between past and present is complex. Where certain critically important elements of tradition are concerned, the dichotomy between past and present vanishes. The inherited prerogatives represented in masks and carvings of crest figures have the same meaning now as they had a century ago.

Native people have expressed concern that traditional museum exhibits, which concentrate only on the past, give a false impression that Native culture and identity existed only in the past. The exhibits developed so far for the houses in the Grand Hall have been developed with a concern to show the connections between the past and present.

In museum exhibits, the particular is made to stand for the general. Non-Native visitors have expressed surprise at the number and variety of houses in the hall. In contrast, Native visitors have found that there are not enough houses in the Grand Hall to fully represent the many different groups of people who make their home on the Pacific Coast and who preserve a vital sense of distinctive identity.

In the years to come, exhibits in the Grand Hall will explore aspects of history and culture belonging to all regions of the coast.

Facing page, *Terry Starr, project supervisor for the Tsimshian house builders, places finishing touches on the Tsimshian house-front painting in June 1989.*
(Photograph: B. McLennan)

Credits

House Builders

Bill McLennan – *Project Coordinator*
  University of British Columbia (U.B.C.)
  Museum of Anthropology

Lyle Wilson – *Project Consultant*
  U.B.C. Museum of Anthropology

Debbie Jeffries – *Project Consultant*
  U.B.C. Museum of Anthropology

Coast Salish House

Joe Becker – *Project Supervisor*
Jack Stogan
Joe Dan Jr.
Clayton Dan
Ramsey Louis
Richard Campbell
Dominic Point – *Elder, consultant*
Shane Point – *Screen painter*

Nuu-Chah-Nulth House

Hudson Webster – *Project Supervisor*
Edgar Charlie
Charlie Lucas
McKenzie Charlie
James Chester
Christine Webster
Ramona Gus
Frank Charlie
Ron Hamilton – *Screen painter, consultant*

Central Coast House

Doug Cranmer – *Project Supervisor*
Bruce Alfred
Al West
Gus Matilpi
Donna Ambers
Hup

Nuxalk House

Glenn Tallio – *Project Supervisor*
Donald Mack
Stirling Tallio
Marvin Tallio

Haida House

Jim Hart – *Project Supervisor*
Bill Lawson
Kenny Davis
Timothy Edgars
John Yeltatzie
Arnie Bellis
Brady Edwards
Henry Dix

Tsimshian House

Terry Starr – *Project Supervisor*
Harry Martin
Mitchell Morrison
Chester Williams
Lawrence Wilson
Victor Reece
Brian Robinson
Henry Green

Modern Works of Art

Raven Bringing Light to the World
   sculpture by Robert Davidson

Coast Salish painting
   Shane Point

Nuu-Chah-Nulth house-front painting
   Ron Hamilton, with the assistance of
   Lyle Wilson

Nuu-Chah-Nulth pole
   Tim Paul
   Art Thompson
   Kevin Cranmer

Wakas house-front painting
   Doug Cranmer
   Bruce Alfred

Wakas pole restoration
   Doug Cranmer
   Bruce Alfred

Dance screen
   Richard Hunt

Button blanket
   Lillian Gladstone

Nuxalk House figures
   Glenn Tallio

Tsimshian house-front painting
   Terry Starr
   Harry Martin
   Chester Williams

Tsonoqua feast dish
   Calvin Hunt

Modern Haida canoe
   Bill Reid

Exhibit Teams

Grand Hall
   George MacDonald
   Ian Gregory
   Andrea Laforet
   Leslie Tepper
   Carole Audet
   David Bevan
   George Nitefor

Kwakwaka'wakw Exhibit
   Gloria Cranmer-Webster
   Ian Gregory
   Andrea Laforet
   Leslie Tepper
   with extensive assistance from
   Davina Hunt

Potlatch Audiovisual Presentation
   Producer's Workshop, Vancouver
   Special thanks are extended to
   Bernard Léveillé.

Nuxalk Exhibit
   Margaret Stott
   Bill McLennan
   David Cunningham
   Leslie Tepper
   Mabel Hall
   Lawrence Pootlass
   Stuart Clellamin
   Karen Anderson
   Willie Hans
   Nuxalk elders

Sustained Technical Assistance
René LeBlanc
Don Groh
Dennis Fletcher
Alan Cottrell
Justin Lencziewski
Margery Toner

Conservation
Virtually every staff member of the Conservation Services Division has worked on projects for the Grand Hall, and their dedication and attention to detail are gratefully acknowledged. Particular assistance has been given by Tom Govier, Charles Hett, James Hay and Martha Segal. In the early days of the development of the hall, considerable work was also done by the Canadian Conservation Institute, particularly on the Sisiutl house posts and the Bear's Den pole.

Scrim

Photography
Bob Destrube

Artwork
Gordon Webber

Technical assistance
throughout the process
David Kingstone
Canadian Government Photo Centre

Acknowledgements

The following people and organizations made particular parts
of the Grand Hall possible through generous gifts:

Raven Bringing Light to the World
   Dr. Margaret P. Hess

The Scrim
   Flexmural Ltée, Montréal, Quebec

The Nuu-Chah-Nulth pole
   The Royal British Columbia Museum

The Kwakwaka'wakw exhibit
   Mr. and Mrs. Eric W. Padgham
   Miss Mabel LeCouvie

References Cited

Barbeau, Marius
1929   *Totem Poles of the Gitksan.* Ottawa:
        National Museum of Canada.
1950   *Totem Poles.* Volumes I and II. Ottawa:
        National Museum of Canada.

Boas, Franz
1921   *Ethnology of the Kwakiutl.* Bureau of American
        Ethnology. Annual Report, 35, pp. 43-1481.

Dalziell, Kathleen
1968   *The Queen Charlotte Islands.* Volume I. 1774-1966.
        Queen Charlotte City, Canada: Bill Ellis, Publisher.

Duff, Wilson
1959   *Histories, Territories and Laws of the Kitwancool.*
        Anthropology in British Columbia, Memoir No. 4.

Halpin, Marjorie
1973   The Tsimshian Crest System: A Study Based on
        Museum Specimens and William Beynon Field Notes.
        Unpublished PhD Dissertation. University of British
        Columbia.

Kew, J.E. Michael
1980   *Sculpture and Engraving of the Coast Salish Indians.*
        U.B.C. Museum of Anthropology. Museum Note No. 9.

MacDonald, George F.
1983   *Haida Monumental Art.* Vancouver: University of British
        Columbia Press.
1984   *The Totem Poles and Monuments of Gitwangak Village.*
        Studies in Archaeology, Architecture and History.
        National Parks and Sites Branch, Parks Canada.
        Environment Canada.

Macnair, Peter, with Alice Paul and other Hesquiaht elders
1989   The Hesquiaht Pole Story. Royal British Columbia
        Museum. Manuscript.

McIlwraith, T.F.
1948   *The Bella Coola Indians.* Toronto:
        University of Toronto Press.

Newcombe, C.F.
n.d.   Collector's Notes. Canadian Museum of Civilization.

Sapir, E.
n.d.   Collector's Notes. Canadian Museum of Civilization.

Smith, Harlan I.
1926   Notes on Totem Poles (of Kitwanga, British Columbia).
        Manuscript. Archaeological Survey of British Columbia.
        Canadian Museum of Civilization.
n.d.   Collector's Notes. Canadian Museum of Civilization.

Swanton, J.R.
1909   *Contributions to the Ethnology of the Haida.*
        Jesup North Pacific Expedition, Vol. V. American
        Museum of Natural History Memoirs 8: 1-300.

The Grand Hall, 1989 (Drawing: G. Webber)

1. Haida Canoe
2. Bear's Den Pole
3. White Squirrel
4. Tsimshian House
5. Kwahsuh Pole
6. Fox Warren Pole
7. Kayang Pole
8. Haida House
9. House Waiting for Property Pole
10. Estuary Environment
11. Chief Wiah's House Post
12. Forest Environment

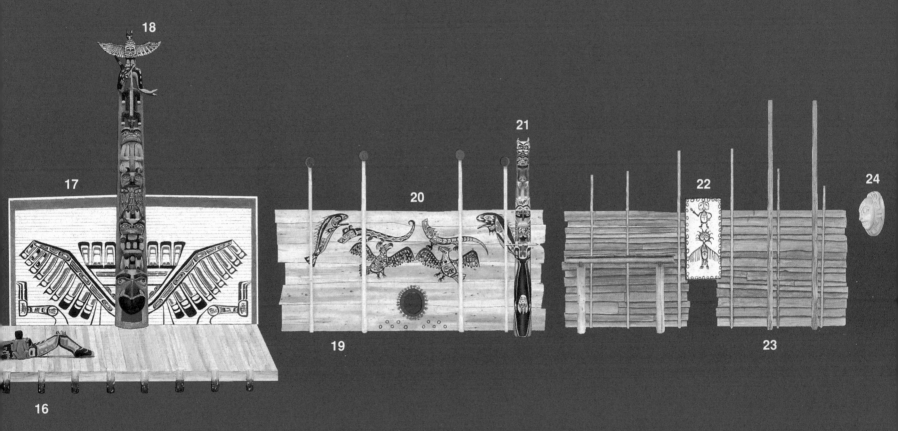

13. Tallio Pole

14. Nuxalk House

15. Chief Qomoqua's Pole

16. Tsonoqua Feast Dish

17. Central Coast House

18. Wakas Pole

19. Summer Shore

20. Nuu-Chah-Nulth House

21. Nuu-Chah-Nulth Pole

22. Coast Salish House

23. Tidal Pool

24. *Raven Bringing Light to the World*